PIER QUEEN

Danielle,
Much love !
Keep writing !
Emanuel Xavier

PIER QUEEN

Emanuel Xavier

Photographs by Richard Renaldi

QUEER MOJO
A Rebel Satori Imprint
Bar Harbor, Maine

ISBN: 978-1-60864-073-7

Printed in the U.S.A.

Rebel Satori Press
P.O. Box 363
Hulls Cove, ME 04644

publication credits

Grateful acknowledgment is made to the following publications in which these poems have previously appeared:

"Bushwick Bohemia" appeared in *Má-Ka- Diasporic Juks: Contemporary Writings by Queers of African Descent,* 1997 (edited by Douglas, McFarlane, Silvera and Stewart), *Urban Latino Magazine*, 1998 and *If Jesus Were Gay & other poems,* 2010 (Rebel Satori Press).

"Every Latino" appeared in *If Jesus Were Gay & other poems,* 2010 (Rebel Satori Press).

"Deliverance" appeared in *Out in Thailand,* 2012 and *If Jesus Were Gay & other poems,* 2010 (Rebel Satori Press).

"Nueva York" appeared in *If Jesus Were Gay & other poems,* 2010 (Rebel Satori Press).

"Abuela's Advice" and "Abuela's Advice #2" appeared in *The James White Review,* 1998.

"Another Country" appeared in *The James White Review,* 1998 and *In Our Own Words: A Generation Defining Itself- Volume 7,* 2007 (edited by Marlow Peerse Weaver).

"Boy Friend" appeared in *XY Magazine,* 1999.

"Sanctuary" appeared in *Poetic Voices,* 1999.

"Oyá/ St. Therese" appeared in *Blood & Tears: Poems for Matthew Shepard*, 1999 (edited by Scott Gibson, Painted

Leaf Press) and *If Jesus Were Gay & other poems,* 2010 (Rebel Satori Press).

"Tradiciones" appeared in *Urban Latino Magazine*, 1998, *phati'tude Literary Magazine,* 1999 and *Long Shot-Volume 25,* 2002, and *If Jesus Were Gay & other poems,* 2010 (Rebel Satori Press).

"Legendary" appeared in *Bullets & Butterflies: queer spoken word poetry*, 2005 (suspect thoughts press) and *If Jesus Were Gay & other poems*, 2010 (Rebel Satori Press).

Contents

It's just another man
holding me close
as we stare out into the Hudson River

Of course, we'd be at the West Side Highway piers
with the moon light shining over New York City

There would most certainly be a soothing, gentle breeze
We wouldn't have to say a single word
No one would bother us

It would just be two guys
a song in our heads
a smile on our faces
and the memory of all who came before

—Emanuel Xavier,
"Love (for lack of a better title)"

This spring is not so beautiful there-
  But dream ships sail away
To where the spring is wondrous rare
  And life is gay.

This spring is not so beautiful there-
  But lads put out to sea
Who carry beauties in their hearts
  And dreams, like me.

—Langston Hughes,
"Water-Front Streets"

DEDICATED TO MY FATHER—
WHEREVER HE MAY BE

INTRODUCTION BY EMANUEL XAVIER

It's been such a journey putting this slim collection together for its first ever publication. *Pier Queen* was self-published in 1997 as a glorified chapbook complete with binding and an ISBN number to get it into bookstores on consignment. Nonetheless, it was still an individual venture inspired by the many great chapbooks I came across at readings from spoken word artists and aspiring poets who had much influence on the development of my own voice and style.

I had just overcome a drug addiction I was too proud to admit I had struggled with and parted ways with the drug dealer I had been working for. It was total social suicide to go from popular NYC club kid to attending poetry workshops. My fascination with vicious drag queens reading the children to filth had shifted to powerful voices speaking about struggle and political awareness. I no longer wanted to disappear into an intoxicated state of mind and an array of shirtless bodies. I needed to confront my reality and deal with my emotions.

I've mentioned in interviews how I had been afraid I might have been HIV positive as I had been a hustler and not always made smart choices in my profession. Though I ended up testing negative and not dying immediately and dramatically after self-publication of this manifesto, the fear was definitely a driving force and a strong presence throughout this collection.

Reading it now, fifteen years later, I come face to face with a really angry and hurt young man looking to leave something behind and make peace with his demons. He is defensive and perhaps limited to the only world he knows. He had no formal education and no ground to stand on as a writer but he was damn ballsy and his ambition was underestimated.

I remember the first time I stepped up to the mic at the Nuyorican Poets Cafe to slam with a poem I had just written titled, "Bushwick Bohemia." It was a Wednesday night and

I was somehow unnerved by the fact I had never done this before. Credit my fellow pier queens who had provided me with a thick skin and loud mouth. I may have been miles from the West Side Highway piers but I still felt at home. That venue brought out something in me long before I even knew who the hell Miguel Piñero or Pedro Pietri was.

I ended up winning my very first slam and going on to compete in the big Friday night Grand Slam showdown hosted by the legendary Keith Roach. I had just enough time to put together a few other options in case I made it to the second and third rounds. Amongst my competitors, I was up against a popular white rapper and the daughter of Nuyorican icon, Sandra Maria Esteves. With the three of us left standing and no foreseeable chance of winning over a notoriously tough crowd, I had decided I would leave them all with a very personal piece of me.

I had only heard rumors of other openly gay poets brazenly sharing their stories in front of audiences at the Nuyorican Poets Cafe but never imagined I would be standing in the spotlight reading the poem "Deliverance" as what I thought would be my early swan song before heading back to the piers.

I ended up winning much to my own dismay and will never forget how much I cried that night as soon as I turned the corner of East 3rd Street and Avenue B. I had never felt so vulnerable and publicly given others access to my deepest secrets and yet felt such relief. I had won. It gave me the inspiration and permission to continue writing and before I knew it, I had a collection of poems I wanted to get published.

I didn't even own a computer. Most of *Pier Queen* was put together in my friend Stephanie's apartment in Harlem. I spent the summer of '97 putting this book together while my friends were either playing handball or hanging out on Christopher Street. For the most part, I didn't really know what I was doing but it was probably one of the happiest times of my life. Through writing, I was learning about myself and by getting it out into the world I was inspiring a new generation of voices to share their own experiences.

We had been ignored and repressed for far too long

and were nothing but mere footnotes in our own history books. Nobody wanted to deal with the children forced to find comfort in the deteriorating piers on the edge of one of the most famous cities in the world. Nobody was interested in crediting us for so many contributions to our culture. Working at a gay bookstore I found close to nothing published that reflected the world I knew existed.

Others supported me, not necessarily because I had great talent, but because they understood the need and desire I had to get noticed as someone who had survived the brutal streets to discover expression through spoken word poetry. Others had come before me but slam poetry had become increasingly popular at the same time I stepped up to the mic and I found myself at the center of it all at the right place and at the right time.

If there was a microphone and the opportunity to read one of my poems in NYC, I was there self-promoting the hell out of this chapbook. I was everywhere I could possibly be, even distributing postcard poems at the clubs and the piers, shamelessly making a name for myself because I knew it was the only way to get noticed.

Though I have never published with a big publishing house or had a publicist, fifteen years later, I can look back and say I've done pretty well for myself. I've done a lot and it's a good time to dust off this collection and officially bring it to print. I don't know exactly what memories this book or any of these poems holds for others but, for me, it heralds the beginning of a great transition in my life from hustling my body to sharing my soul. It hasn't made me rich. It hasn't made me famous. It has made me proud to say I conquered my own demons.

Emanuel Xavier
NYC, 2012

AFTER THE BALL
Emanuel Xavier Exits the Club Scene and Pens a Classic

Foreword by Rigoberto Gonzalez

The raw details of Emanuel Xavier's early years are widely known. He claimed his troubled past and crafted it into the art that has made him a popular performer and populist poet since *Pier Queen* made its first appearance in print back in 1997:

> *Tell me about how I ended up*
> *Hustling on the streets of Nueva York*
> *Befriending drug dealers and prostitutes*
> *Homeless transsexuals giving me a House*
> *In this promised land*
> *This American dream*

The act of writing is likely what saved him—citizens of the queer community know the destructive force of the demons that seize us in our youth and what it takes to overcome them. And those who survive, Manny's work tells us, have the responsibility to bear witness on behalf of those who don't: "all the sisters are dying/ all our legends are dead."

Though *Pier Queen* provides snapshots of the queer scene of the 80s and 90s, back when Manhattan had street cred, before Mayor Rudolph Giuliani cleaned up the once-edgy Times Square and turned it into a tourist hot-spot with aberrations like M & M's World, the book's gaze is actually upon Brooklyn's poor immigrant Latino neighborhoods, where young gay men of color struggle with a dual life. One is informed by the masculine codes of behavior demanded by their Latino households; the other by their private desires.

The ability to navigate from one culture to another is paralleled by the journey between Brooklyn and Manhattan, and no side provides complete fulfillment or refuge for the queer Latino. But from this comes a double-edged power: banjee realness. The phrase "banjee realness" was a category of drag prominently featured in the 1990 documentary *Paris is Burning*, which was the nation's glimpse into the New York City ball scene. Banjee referred to the homoeroticized image of urban working class black/ Latino masculinity—a sought-after commodity that could also be exploited ("Walk hard with a slight limp for allure.") by those who could provide it:

> *I sell myself to faggots*
> *wrinkled, old faggots*
> *stupid amounts of cash*
> *for a taste of banjee heaven.*

And from the poem "Bushwick Bohemia":

> *Up on the roof,*
> *Miguelito giving blowjobs*
> *to grey-haired old men*
> *so that he can get a fade at Paul's boutique*
> *or buy mami that fake painting*
> *she wanted for $5.99*
> *down Knickerbocker Avenue*

Transactions between the "banjee hustler boy" and the white man trick illuminate a series of planes that give Manny's poems depth: sexuality, race/ ethnicity, class and even language are in simultaneous dialogue, naming a problematic sexual dynamic that is directly critiqued, questioned, and confronted. But what's most relevant about this communication is that it's voiced by the banjee boy himself, transforming the object of desire into a realized subject:

> *I ain't no Hooked-On-Phonics cha-cha queen*
> *here to wash your dishes, shine your shoes,*
> *take your orders, serve your food,*
> *teach you dirty words in Spanish*
> *like "puta," "sucia." "asquerosa"*

so that you could curse me in my own language
when you realize I have absolutely no intention
of being your banjee boy fantasy
Ay papi, ay papi, Puh-lease!

If the Latino's queer landscapes (the streets, the clubs) are fraught with conflict, so too is his home. Manny writes with sensitivity about the poverty of his childhood neighborhood, keeping *Pier Queen* bound to its cultural roots:

Papito vendiendo coquitos
mientras brown-skinned project mothers
cross themselves every morning
before heading off to the factories
or going out to do the compras
so that the children won't have to eat
pan con welfare cheese again.

Yet with the same breath he's unafraid to reveal the abuse and heartache of family dysfunction, as in the poem "Deliverance," a piece addressed to a father who abandoned his child. This touching dramatic monologue is heavy with emotion, its gravity speaking to the dangerous hierarchies (father, father-figure, mother, child) sustained by distressed and broken households:

Padre, perdóname
for trying to kill off mami & her boyfriend
pouring bleach into their soup
thinking maybe he won't beat her no more
maybe she won't beat me no more
No mas, mami, no mas
because I remind her of you.

"Race, class and sexuality" has become somewhat of a scholarly catch-phrase since American literature can now boast an extensive body of work that explores this nexus. But it's important to note that Emanuel Xavier's *Pier Queen* was a trailblazing early example for the newest generation of queer Latino writers. If ever art was a gesture of courage and activism, then there is no clearer evidence—this self-published collection of poetry that launched a career, and, more importantly, that established a precedent for Latino writers born after 1970.

I salute Manny on the occasion of this official publication, with gratitude for setting in motion the next phase of queer Latino letters. There is no turning back and no apology for moving forward. Indeed, he has shown us how to be forthright, how to be fierce.

Rigoberto González
New York City, 2012

BANJEE REALNESS

BUSHWICK BOHEMIA

Para mi gente...
chequealo...
Bushwick on my mind
quinceañeras at the *bodega*
with their pretty pink dresses
luscious dark eyes
longing to cut the Valencia cakes
while Mr. Softee lingers
over *coco helados y piragüeros*
fighting for the last dollar

Across the street,
santeros dressed in white
with their *collares*
buying chickens at the poultry shop
for their next *tambor*
to be held this Sunday
in someone else's crowded basement

Maggie cruisin' back and forth
back and forth
Keeping the dealers in check
As the sounds of beepers
Rottweiler fights
Freestyle
& chanting from the Pentecostal church
fill the air with the smells
of *pernil, alcapurrias y empanadas*
from La Claribel -
the best *cuchifrito* in town

Up on the roof,

Miguelito giving blowjobs
to grey-haired old men
so that he can get a fade
at Paul's boutique
or buy mami that fake painting
she wanted for $5.99
down Knickerbocker Avenue

Malitza walking by
pregnant with her second baby
only 18 & already night manager at McDonald's
She wasn't gonna end up consumed
in the empty little crack bags
she counted
every morning
on her way to Grover Cleveland High School

Hector, her boyfriend,
home from playing handball all day
lying shirtless on the couch blunted out of his mind
staring at the roach on the ceiling
one single roach in a vast desert
or maybe an alien exploring a new world
the ceiling fan -
his spaceship

Doña Carmen sneezing so loud
The walls so thin
Hector says *'Salud'*
& she hears him from the second floor
over Walter Mercado
on *Canal 41*

Turning off the kitchen lights
so that the roaches can scurry into the darkness -
their freedom

like the children playing out all night

Waiting for the L train
'*Mira,* Georgie...
gimmie a quarter!'
'Fine...
but cha betta pay me back tomorrow!'

Life in Bushwick,
ain't it a trip!
One day we'll all be buried
beneath the ground we spit on

PIER QUEEN RADIO BLUES

Flying high above the Hudson River
the tranquility—tingly, crystal-like sensations
as Heaven's Gates appear through big, fluffy clouds

Hello? You are on the air!

St. Peter . . . What's going on girl?
My name is Terence LaBeija-Xtravaganza-Dupri
& you would WANT to have me on the guest-list!

Hello? You are on the air!

My face is cracked
standing alone in a desert
motorcycles speeding by
the faucets 'drip-drip' dripping
feeding my anxiety as the end approaches

Hello? ...

I KNOW ALREADY, I AM ON THE FUCKIN' AIR!
GOD IS LOVE, LOVE IS GOD- WHATEVER!
I'VE NEVER BEEN PAST CHRISTOPHER!
Mama swallowed a bullet back at the piers
& I learned that there is beauty in darkness
but more beauty in sound

Hello? You are on the air!

If I were to travel through your subconscious,
would you wait for me?
WILL YOU WAIT FOR ME?

4

Hello . . . you are on the air-

BACK UP BITCH!
If I were to . . . St. Peter . . . speeding by . . .
I AM ON THE GUEST-LIST!
I SWEAR!

Hello? You are on the air!

TRANCE

The B A S S
in your voice
vibrates
within the realms
of my mind
body
and S O O O U L
provoking the selfish dreams
of an inner child
unsettled
unashamed

SLEEPING IN SUBWAYS

cold, hard seats comfort me
about as much as the walls of your touch
the irritating crash of rusted metal cutting into my heart
with the memories of your jagged, mystifying voice

quickly dodging my watering eyes
from the perverted death and bitter yawns of unfriendly
    strangers
desperately trying to fall unconscious with delusions of
    happiness
while traffic jams bellow inside of me
like the noisy, overcrowded streets above
longing to be held in your violent distance
only so that i could slowly fade
leaving you
the least bit untouched

just another lonely subway station
lurking mysteriously in my rat infested underground
waiting for these sadomasochistic feelings
to stumble into your cruel, sadistic cars
with hopes of one day waking up
to rise from this twisted darkness
and hail a fuckin' taxi cab instead

LOVE IS THE MESSAGE

Everybody say "Love"

I love you so much but I couldn't tell you because I was
    afraid to lose you

I love you so fuckin' much but I need to have sex with other
    people
to remind me of how much I love you

I love you and I'm so sorry that I bashed your face in
but you really pissed me off when I came home and dinner
    wasn't ready

Shut the fuck up and let me fuck you without a condom
to show you just how much I fucking love you

Baby, baby, baby I love you but you gotta go before my wife
    comes home

I love you just the way you are but you've got to go to the
    gym and work out,
otherwise I can't be seen with you

I love you and I'm sorry I stole your credit cars and your car
but, *mira papi,* I love myself more

I love you all for loving me

I love you. You love me. We're both high on ecstasy.

L-O-V-E. It's all about love.

REALNESS
(RETRO BANJEE)

1. For baseball caps, use a beer can to curve the bill into an oval shape giving you those dark, concealing features.
2. Jeans must be worn extra baggy and low enough to show off those sexy boxer shorts. Cuff the bottom over boots and sneakers. Shorts always long enough to cover the kneecaps. Never accentuate the booty by wearing anything tight. Once again- Never accentuate the booty!
3. Important accessories include: beepers (functioning or otherwise), nose rings, goldcaps, tattoos, rolling paper and tweezers.
4. Never smile at strangers, particularly when walking behind old ladies so as to make them clutch their purses. Shades are preferable and essential to enhancing attitude, especially after a long night of drinking '40's and getting weeded.
5. Walk hard with a slight limp for allure. Canes are exceptionally convincing. Never strut or bounce as weapons and drugs might drop to the ground.
6. Never reference the police as "cops" as they may be right around the corner. Give them names like "Maggie" or "Angie." For example- *Chill, Maggie's down the block!* This way they'll think you are talking about some girl and not get suspicious.

BANJEE HUSTLER BOY

I sell myself to faggots
wrinkled, old faggots
stupid amounts of cash
for a taste of banjee heaven
destroying happy homes
expensive bedsheets
white bedsheets
(always white bedsheets)
soaking up humiliation, deprivation, guilt
consuming blood, spirit, soul
sometimes the bathroom, sometimes a blow
savoring cum shooting over my tongue
pulling out Blow Pops
to sabotage the foul, ridiculed loneliness

So wha'cha, wha'cha, wha'cha want?

Cha want love? Cha want attention?
Don't even mention
'cause I ma cut cha
hungry face
begging for love
getting infections

Do you really give a fuck? About your wife? Your kids?
Your dog? Your dollars?
Loca, please!
When the ship leaves, another one docks this harbor

Who's the powerless one?

EVERY LATINO

Every Latino
carries a switchblade
in their back pocket
ready to cut cha
if you just look at them the wrong way
years of hunger and discrimination
piercing through their jaded eyes

Every Latino
cheats on their girlfriends
boyfriends
(or both)
marries only when the condom breaks
lives off welfare
ritually watching *telenovelas*
while Walter Mercado predictions
forecast their million dollar Lotto dreams

Every Latino
lives in some greasy apartment
smoking too much pot
where even the roaches smoke roaches
getting drunk outside
brightly lit bodegas
wives in the kitchen cooking all day

Every Latino
wears thick stolen gold chains
San Lazaro or Santa Barbara
hanging against tanned Sazón flavored chests
the smell of herbs reeking
from their spicy criminal skins

Every Latino
is only good as a delivery boy
dishwasher
waiter
stock boy
hustler

Every Latino
believes in and practices Santeria
killing chickens with bare hands
drinking their blood like Kool-Aid
candles lit for every occasion
to plaster statues of every saint known to mankind
including deceased family members and friends

Every Latino
is Puerto Rican if you live in New York
Mexican if you live in Texas or California
Cuban if you live in Florida
Doesn't matter where we're from
in their eyes
WE'RE ALL THE FUCKIN' SAME

PARADISE

I dreamed that I died
and was on the list to the fiercest club
above
where drugs are free
angels float on ecstasy
posing lavishly
on disco-ball clouds
to the wicked sounds
of Our Heavenly Father

Chillin' with my main man, Jesus
He says to me
AND HE SAYS TO ME
Yo, wassup, kid? You wanna smoke up?
Uppity up
Passing me the big phat blunt
wrapped tightly in rolling paper
made from the cross

Weeded,
I says to Him
AND I SAYS TO HIM
Yo, Jee! Am I in heaven?
Choking on a mad puff
He looks at me
incredulously
ready to snap and read
Ms. Thing, AT ALL! This is Sound Factory!

Then Mary in a K-hole walks toward me
walks for me
doin' the K-walk

doin' the runway
in her red patent leather high heel stilettos
offering me a bump
Bumpity bump
a chunk
of paradise
and I knew I was in heaven

LETTER TO THE MAYOR

for Rudy Giuliani

Dear Mr. Mayor,

Sir, I write you this letter to let you know you have ruined
    my life—
the life of my brothers, the life of my sisters,
the life of this city.
If we band together
and move rhythmically at K mart,
would you *please* close it down too?
If the hookers dressed up like Esmeralda,
The Little Mermaid, Cinderella,
If we were to buy ecstasy with Lion King, Aladdin, Hercules
    imprints,
would we finally be accepted into your "quality of life"?
Please Mr. Mayor, please let me be part of your dream.
I'll put on my Mickey Mouse ears, pretend I am three again
and let Captain Eo rape and fuck me like Pocahontas's land
until I bleed the color of Snow White's apple
and cum 101 "family value" Dalmatians
so I could grow up to be
the perfect Disney minority salesman I was meant to be.
No dysfunctions. No delusions.
Just Donald Duck, Goofy, Pluto and me.
Please, Mr. Mayor.
Pretty, pretty please.

                        Sincerely,
                        Mikey X.

INSOMNIA

toss and turn
toss and turn
pillows no longer comfort me
all alone
without you by my side
waiting hopelessly
to get you off my mind
to sleep
to dream
to awaken
to happiness

toss and turn
toss and turn
darkness cannot conceal loneliness
no one to hold
no one to awaken
no one to toss and turn
from guilt
from fear
from emptiness

except myself
all alone
without you by my side

Tomorrow I'll try NyQuil

WINDCHIMES

The moon reaches its final eclipse
shadows fall upon The Earth
the apocalyptic winds of Oyá
breeze through the prophecy of birth
evil haunting bitter souls
love never a stranger
Soon friends will laugh, poets will dance
misery will be endangered

RELIGIOUS CIRCLES

What goes around
comes around
round and round
until you are wrapped
coiled in fate

gâtãy gâtãy para-gâtãy
para-sâhm-gâtãy

Gone, gone, gone
Safely passed to the other shore

Yet something's missing
something's not said
searching these rivers for expressions of beauty
drowning in anger, perversion, contempt
Santos sailing through the salsa music of my soul
with the strength and power of Vishnu
chanting prayers from faraway lands

gâtãy gâtãy para-gâtãy
para-sâhm-gâtãy

God, Buddha, Obbatala- I do not know what to call you
I do not care what to call you
because in my tropical storms I feel your presence
In my tropical storms I am not alone

bõdee svâ-hâ

So be it

DELIVERANCE

Padre, perdóname
but where were you when I was three
getting fucked up the ass by my oldest cousin
Palabras reminding me
IF YOUR MAMI FINDS OUT,
SHE'LL LEAVE YOU
LIKE YOUR DADDY DID!
                  . . . like your daddy did
. . . like daddy did
leaving behind a curious child
kicking preschool teachers in the crotch
smashing up aquariums
watching enviously
pretty little goldfish
struggling desperately for air
dying slowly
helplessly
like myself

Padre, perdóname
for trying to kill off mami & her boyfriend
pouring bleach into their soup
thinking maybe he won't beat her no more
maybe she won't beat me no more
No mas, mami, no mas
because I remind her of you
with my pearl-black eyes
     my darker skin
     my differences

Padre, perdóname
for running away at 16

mami running after me barefoot
over broken glass
her legs left bloodied & blue
out on my own
lying to get by
stealing to feed the hunger
selling my soul
to the brutal pleasures
of wrinkled old men
wrinkled and old like my daddy
hoping one day to wake up in your arms
whispering how much you love me
needing anyone to love me

Padre, perdóname
for poisoning myself
with powders, herbs & pills
used to forget
that you abandoned me
when I woke up
throwing up
charcoal
in front of that nurse
wanting only to die
left only to cry
ma mí
     ma
       mí
Por favor, perdóname

but real men never cry
mami says *faggots deserve to die*

Wiping myself
staring at the blood
       shit

                    scum
from the last trick
that once again
left me bruised
deep inside

Padre, perdóname
for breathing
for living
for wondering
                where you are
                what your eyes look like
After all, I'm still your son
I'm still your little boy
Aren't I?
Daddy

BUTCH QUEEN IN HIGH HEELS

CHELSEA QUEEN

for Cliff

So you *think* you are *fieeerce*?
With your gym memberships, steroid enhanced bitch tits,
tight ass daisy duke shorts, circuit parties, and drug
    addictions?

Well, let me tell you a little sumethin' sumethin' about being
    fieeerce!
Looking at me looking at you looking at me looking at you
with that stupid look on your face

I ain't no Hooked-On-Phonics cha-cha queen
here to wash your dishes, shine your shoes,
take your orders, serve your food,
teach you dirty words in Spanish
like *"puta", "sucia", "asquerosa"*
so that you could curse me in my own language
when you realize I have absolutely no intention
of being your banjee boy fantasy
Ay papi, ay papi, Puh-lease!

But enough about me, let's talk about you
Impressing yourself with Ralph, Tommy, and Calvin
purchased in the right baggy oversizes
The right baseball caps concealing the decadence of your
    frustration
while trying to keep up to my tribal beats
without any rhythm, soul or, like you say, *"sabrosura"*

Imagining yourself open-minded with a trip to

the latest gay latino club
to pick up some "hot pieces" to bend over and fuck
with your white supremacist bullshit

Ay papi, ay papi, Puh-lease!
Keep cloning yourself into oblivion
Keep bench pressing yourself with prejudice
Keep injecting yourself with ignorance
But, whatever you do *papi*, don't you evah forget
the color of the cock you like the best!

NUEVA YORK

While Mexicans shine the soul of the white man's shoes
Ricans and Dominicans drive around
with black-faced virgins and saints on their dashboards
blasting rap and freestyle
down the streets where mountain campesinos
fall in love with South American cholas
getting cruised by the homeless men
loose change jingling in their pockets

All the latinos freezing their nalgas off screaming
ME CAGO EN DIOS!
while reminiscing about homelands
where tropical trees and twilight's warm their souls
& the sun brings out natural skin tones

Papito vendiendo coquitos
mientras brown-skinned project mothers
cross themselves every morning
before heading off to the factories
or going out to do the compras
so that the children won't have to eat
pan con welfare cheese again

16-year-old Angie popping her gum
hands on her cintura
screaming
Yo Miriam...Throw down the baby!
but I don't wanna go up the stairs...I'm too tired!
Just throw the baby out the window...I'll catch him!
I SWEAR!

The gringos

watching curiously
lost in the translation
unable to understand
the slang bodega terms
the Nuyorican words
that give the spice of life
el ritmo y el sabor
to la isla del encanto
to la isla de Nueva York

ENAMORADO

late at night
after all the children have fallen asleep
after all the lullabies have been sung
the stars glow fiercely
promising
we will be together
someday
somewhere
etched forever
into the rhythms
of our lives

Siempre estaré soñando de ti
no importa adonde,
ni con quien estès,
porque algùn dìa
serè dueño de tu amor
como la lluvia, como el arco iris, como la flor

I will always have you inside my heart
even if you resist the hidden truths revealed in my touch
the secret poems written in my eyes
to do the things that you must do
to keep from falling
          falling
                  falling in love

DESTINY

If
you were to come back to me
I would strip
my arrogance
stroke
your wisdom
leave
you twisted
raw
always exciting
shave
you with jagged edges
silly little lies
dress
the wounds
of our delusional bliss
pose
outside East Village bathhouses, bars
in psychotic embraces
Japanese tourists
curiously capturing
strange behaviors
genuine smiles
deep
in our deviance
diving
into darkness
drowning
in our destiny
because true love is so
hard
to find

ABUELA'S ADVICE

"Always keep two candles lit
So, if one blows out,
you'll have the other one
to light your way
Pero, no mas que dos!
Otherwise, you'll start a fire!"

ABUELA'S ADVICE #2

"Take an orange
Split in two
On a piece of paper write your name
On another piece of paper write her name
Place each piece of paper on top of an orange halve
Pour sugar, honey, molasses, anything sweet over each
Then put the orange together
Tie with a red ribbon
Light yellow candles for Oshún
That oughtta sweeten her up!
It is a 'she' isn't it?
Isn't it?"

ANOTHER COUNTRY

Madre,
Don't tell me
about the poverty
in South America
How cousin Cecilia doesn't have clothes to wear
How screaming babies cry from hunger and thirst
Tell me
about how I ended up
Hustling on the streets of *Nueva York*
Befriending drug dealers and prostitutes
Homeless transsexuals giving me a House
In this promised land
This American dream
This American dream that is a nightmare
when you hold on
to the old-fashioned conservative ideals of distant countries
Where men cannot possibly love men
Where women cannot possibly love women
Where blacks are the enemy
Where whites are the enemy
Where Asians are the enemy
Where other Latinos are the enemy
I am the enemy
Daddy was the enemy
He left you
He left me
I left you
because you left me
screaming
alone
in this promised land

Madre,
Don't tell me
about how happy and perfect
I could have been
had I been raised in South America
Where there is supposedly no such thing as homosexuality
promiscuity, unwed mothers, abortions
Tell me about the women in Peru
forced to marry their rapists
Tell me about the *maricones* in Colombia
that are acceptably beaten to death
Tell me about the blacks in Ecuador
that are considered the lowest form of life
if considered at all
Tell me about the real horrors of third world countries
Where houses crumble to the earth quakes of poverty
Where mothers are beaten by their husbands
Where teenagers kill themselves every day
Where children are raped by their elders
Where crime runs rampant
Where God kills indiscriminately
just like in New York
just like in the United States
just like anywhere you go

Madre,
Somewhere else is not safer
the third world
the second world
the first world
No matter where you go, no matter where you are
It's all the same world
It's just another country

CLUB KID

Dancing
beneath glaring stars
blaring disco lights
casting bodies
in colors of red, green, blue
putting out cigarettes
with platform shoes
Drugs enhancing the celebration of life
flirting with potential 'pieces', husbands, one night delights
'Bumping' white powder clumps with white powder
    clumped drag queens
in bathroom stalls, behind DJ booths
Snuffly pipes- the latest tools
entertaining Generation X- *Xtrava*
Why do we get fucked by the police?
Officer, I can't get no sleep 'cause your nightstick is up my
    ass
shoved in way too deep
I gotta go
I gotta go
I gotta go
I just got a beep

BOY FRIEND

i want to
pass you silly poems on restaurant napkins
reveal to you my darkest secrets and dreams
feel your warm breath going down my neck
run my hands through your shaved head
fall asleep on your chest under a full moon
wake up to the nostalgia of bad breath
smell the sweet intoxication of private parts
get high with you on every stoop in the city
steal kisses from you in subway stations
slap you on the back of the head for cruising
wear your clothes and dress you up in mine
bathe you in spiritual cleansing herbs and oils
leave the club scene for the white picket fence
raise cows, chickens, and pigs
buy fruits at the market
walk around holding your hand- sticky, damp, sweet
watch movies in the theater with you smack in the center
enjoying Surround Sound
while feeding you warm, buttery popcorn
gloating to all my friends
over and over and over again
about how much I love you
just you
only you
nobody else
just you
but God damn it! *Maldita sea!*
You just had to be straight!

XTRAVAGANZA

X
X
X
Xtrava
pier cruisin'
blunt smokin'
forty drinkin'
trick hustlin'
cock suckin'
finger snappin'
gum chewin'
shade poppin'
hair pinnin'
face beatin'
bitch slappin'
knife cuttin'
store moppin'
list workin'
drug snortin'
ball walkin'
hip hoppin'
vogue posin'
Paris burnin'
House battlin'
floor servin'
trophy snatchin'
motherfuckin'
ganza

LOST IN TRANSLATION

for Cheryl Boyce-Taylor

Bring me a white boy who swears he is Latino
and I will make him eat *pasteles, bacalao, carne guisada*
    con yucca y tostones
Sew his ass cheeks together
Force feed him *maltas y batidos de papaya*
    con leche de Carnation (of course)
Watch his belly explode into a million fatherless babies,
poverty crushed dreams and overcrowded ghettos
where police sirens nurse children to sleep

Bring me a white boy who swears he is Latino
and I will snatch him away from his corporate office
and his rich mommy and daddy
Degrade him to a minimum wage job
    where the janitors and factory workers
are his new brothers and sisters and aunts and uncles
Struggling to buy the same designer labels usually charged
    on credit cards
Trading in his fancy family home for a roach-infested,
    no heat apartment
His only worry not whether to visit Becky at the mall
but if he could make it alive to work the next day

Bring me a white boy who swears he is Latino
Bring me a Latino who swears he is a white boy
Bring me any Latino who denies their culture and heritage
and I will bitch slap him with reality
because when trying to be something that you're not
there's always something lost in the translation

38

LOVE BREAK

No more secret recordings of your snores at night
Broken promises, hidden truths, useless fights
Memories- a series of torn pictures, inspiration and love
drowned out by the tears of sacrificed doves
Flying high in search of oceans and pearls
while you live deceived within sheltered wombs
Happiness blinded by disco lights, chattering folk
laughing about loneliness, smiles and words that you spoke
Time revealing the bitter contempt of your sorry goodbyes
No more secret recordings of your cheating and lies

AWAKENING

Wake up, Mikey!
Wake up!
This wicked world was not created for you alone
Time is slipping through your mortal hands
Every breath could be the last

The body of Angel Melendez ...

Wake up, Mikey!
Wake up!
If you run fast enough, the winds of Oyá will not catch you
If you hide within toxic rivers, your thick skin will survive

... low life drug dealer ...

Wake up, Mikey!
Wake up!
Feel the warmth of the sun
Crush the head of the dragon
Pound him with the weight of your existence

... was found in the Hudson River ...

Wake up, Mikey!
Wake up!
Rise from nocturnal silence
Battle beyond ballrooms
Fight the steady pulse of urban decay

... arms and legs cut off

Wake up, Mikey!

Wake up!
Mikey, wake up!
Wake up!
Your disco nap is over

SANCTUARY

Seduced by the enchantment of darkness
evil prevails over children
snatching them loose
from mother's frightened, tight embraces
Carrying away innocence with candles glowing
to taste the blood which flows through virgin veins
splattering three-year-old trails of confusion and pain
over abused mattresses
Isolating them from all others
with a touch
never too simple, too much
leaving behind the dim light of empty souls
while crucified men watch from hollowed walls
Unable to lunge off
destroy the beast
piercing
deep within

I will never forget what you did to me
I will never forget what you did to me
I will never forget what you did to me
I will never forget

Time heals nothing

OYÁ/ST. THERESE

Your womb is the death which surrounds me
the skull I rest at your feet
the candles which make you glow ominously
the mask which disguises deceit
Blessed white doves
I will never be
sailing in the sanctuary
of your mystifying winds
casting lilies from the cobalt skies
high above perversions and sins
Thorned and nailed
I will never be
hanging naked from the wooden cross
clutched fervently
in your bloodied hands-
splintered
bruised
miserably lost
In my heart there is only anger
In my voice there is only pain
Life has taught me I am not a master
Love has taught me I am but a slave
& all I need is deliverance
from the darkness of my grave

AFTER THE BALL

I search for laughter
down an empty Christopher Street
remembering innocent smiles
with every used condom
every vial
of crack
never looking back

but all the sisters are dying
all the legends are dead
our sanctuary closed
always living on the edge

Children floating by
on the Hudson
love is the message
still lingering
in their vacant eyes

Winds call out my name
but I will not listen

I will stay behind

TRADICIONES

I want to break tradition
about latín machismo
fucking every puta in sight
leaving behind nine million, billion children
scattered throughout Brooklyn, Manhattan, the Bronx
marrying the most humble, convenient wife
then cheating on her
beating her
whenever the gandules are too cold-
forget about the chuletas

I want to break tradition-
respecting elders que no me respetan
keeping in touch with distant relatives
that don't give a flying coño about me
because blood is supposed to be thicker than arroz con dulce
but you see- my friends are my family
because they love and accept mis locuras
and don't consider me
una desgracia de la familia

I want to break tradition-
distrusting all blancos
because they do not speak the language
or know how to dance salsa or merengue
Sin embargo, everyone on those telenovelas
has el pelo pintado rubio and green contacts
trying to be la nueva Rita Hayworth or Raquel Welch
adopting supremacist beliefs

I mean, when was the last time you saw a morena
playing anything other than the maid

on Canal 41 o 47?

I want to break tradition-
the mentiras my parents told me about
negros
chinos
gringos
maricónes
cachaperas
Smashing it against the ground
like coconuts
because mi tierra, mi patria es mi barrio
where our Spanish eyes are not blinded by prejuicios
where la única palabra that we do not understand
is hate
y que siga...
y que siga la tradición
bajo la luna, maybe
pero no en el corazón

LEGENDARY

There are Gods amongst us in these ghettos
so black, so fierce,
so brown, so beautiful,
Their time on earth may be as oppressive as ignorance
limited to the demons flowing in their blood
but after safely passing over back to the clouds
the wind will still carry their auras and prophecies
their bones will still beat drums
for their children to dance
the phoenix will still rise from the flames of Paris
with hope in womb

There are Gods amongst us in these ghettos
so brown, so fierce,
so black, so beautiful,
If you spend too much time caught up in yourself
You just might miss Him that is goddess,
She that is god, they that are legends
Working the runway as if walking on water
Reaching the stage to that promised land
where 'peace' is not ridiculed
and the only war worth fighting for
is protecting your child from the terrorist acts
of a mainstream America
where 'reading' is an act of learning
not degrading words used to disguise fragility
and fractured dreams
where 'shade' is a shadow you walk in
to avoid the light
but who wants to stay out of the warmth of the sun?

If you waste your time trying to be a false prophet

robed in attitude and labels to obscure the insecurity
you may fail to recognize their divinity and miracles
parting the crowds, resurrecting from the floor,
scoring tens of commandments,
because trophies will not feed the hungry,
coat the homeless; hide the scars
Grand Prizes will not bring Lazarus or LaBeija
back from the dead
they will just sit in your closet,
fake idols gathering dust,
before the gold paint chips away
You cannot sell them for freedom
You cannot trade them in for love

There are Gods amongst us in these ghettos
so black, so fierce,
so black, so beautiful,
so brown, so fierce,
so brown, so beautiful,
Watch them carefully and say your prayers
as they enter the ballroom
angel wing feathers decorating skin
re-crafted over silicone and martyred colors
See the Gods dream; see the Gods give;
see the Gods live,
They exist in the spaces where white
is not the only hue that represents purity
They will not battle to your rhythms and beats
click, spin, and dip simply for amusement
They will not teach those
who share their souls and names to hate
Their heartbeats are louder than the blaring speakers

You want realness . . . look at your hands
are they red from the revolution?
or from the blood of your own sisters

There are Gods amongst us in these ghettos
so black, so brown, so fierce, so beautiful,
so bright
Look up towards the heavens and pray
then look at yourself in the mirror and say
'Stars are not only found out in the sky
but in ourselves'

I would like to first and foremost thank my wonderful fans and friends that have supported my work throughout the years and helped make this official publication possible.

Much love and gratitude to Sven Davisson and Rebel Satori Press for pulling this title out of obscurity and making it possible for new readers to experience. Thanks to Richard Renaldi for his wonderful photographic collaboration and capturing the beauty of the West Side Highway piers throughout the years.

Stephanie Holley—Girl! Remember when I was using your computer up in Harlem to self-publish the chapbook version of this because I couldn't afford my own? Thanks for giving a pier queen a chance to turn his life around.

Leonardo Toro and Rodney Allen Trice- you guys are the BFF's everyone should have in their lives and I'm not just saying that because of all the unspeakable things you bitches have been part of.

Shelly Weiss and OUTmedia and all the colleges and universities that have invited me to share my work with their students- thanks for giving me the opportunity to be heard and inspire others.

To my beautiful mom—we've had such a journey and yet we managed to pull through. Others are not as lucky and I thank you for encouraging me to speak my truth without holding back.

To Willi Ninja- I miss you so much and know you are smiling down on me with your snaggletooth.

To all my House brothers and 'sistas' and all LGBTQ children everywhere- never stop dreaming and believing that someday there will be a better world for all of us. It really does get better!

CPSIA information can be obtained at www.ICGtesting.com
Printed in the USA
BVOW071426110512

290018BV00001B/4/P